SAMURAI

SAMURAI

ODYSSEYS

RACHAEL HANEL

CREATIVE EDUCATION · CREATIVE PAPERBACKS

Published by Creative Education and Creative Paperbacks
P.O. Box 227, Mankato, Minnesota 56002
Creative Education and Creative Paperbacks
are imprints of The Creative Company
www.thecreativecompany.us

Design by Graham Morgan
Art direction by Tom Morgan

Images by Alamy Stock Photo/North Wind Picture Archives, cover, 17; Getty Images/Bettmann, 11, Hulton Deutsch, 52, Sepia Times, 70–71, Universal History Archive, 32–33, Werner Forman, 40; Unsplash/Nagy Arnold, 50; Wikimedia Commons/A.Davey, 75, Auckland Museum Collections, 29, C. Nakagawa, 58, Felice Beato, 22, 24, 26, Félix Jean Gauchard, 49, https://www.historyoffighting.com/the-blog/category/Art, CC BY-SA 4.0, 37, Kusakabe Kimbei, 12, Mathew Benjamin Brady, 64, public domain, 18, Rabe!, 6, Shinichi Suzuki, 44, Ueno Hikoma, 4–5, Utagawa Yoshikazu, 8, Wellcome Images, 2, Yoshitoshi, 61

Library of Congress Cataloging-in-Publication Data
Names: Hanel, Rachael, author.
Title: Samurai / Rachael Hanel.
Description: Mankato, Minnesota : Creative Education and Creative Paperbacks, [2026] | Series: Odysseys in combat | Includes bibliographical references and index. | Audience: Ages 12–15 years | Audience: Grades 7–9 | Summary: "Prepare for battle alongside the highly respected warriors of Japan called samurai by learning about their weapons, combat skills, and reasons for fighting. Includes a glossary, sidebars, index, and further resources"—Provided by publisher.
Identifiers: LCCN 2024049695 (print) | LCCN 2024049696 (ebook) | ISBN 9798889896500 (lib. bdg.) | ISBN 9781682778166 (paperback) | ISBN 9798889897309 (ebook)
Subjects: LCSH: Samurai—Japan—History—Juvenile literature. | Bushido—Japan—Juvenile literature. | Kendo—Japan—Juvenile literature. | Hand-to-hand fighting, Oriental—Juvenile literature. | Seppuku—Juvenile literature.
Classification: LCC DS827.S3 H36 2026 (print) | LCC DS827.S3 (ebook) | DDC 952—dc23/eng/20241231
LC record available at https://lccn.loc.gov/2024049695
LC ebook record available at https://lccn.loc.gov/2024049696

Printed in India

Museum display of a samurai uniform

CONTENTS

Introduction **9**

The Rise of the Warrior **13**

Early Fighters 18

Men of Many Names 24

A Vicious Way to Fight **27**

Put to the Test 37

Supply and Demand 39

Ready for Attack **41**

Way of the Sword 44

Life and Death 50

The Bravest and the Best **53**

Art Subjects 55

Amakusa Shiro 61

End of an Era **63**

Folded Gifts 70

What's for Dinner? 75

Selected Bibliography **76**

Glossary **77**

Websites **79**

Index **80**

武田大膳大夫信玄
山形三郎兵衛
内藤修理亮
米倉丹後守
一寿斎芳員画
改
子四
柿嵜和泉守
甘利左エ門
今井伊勢守
原大隅

Introduction

From the beginning of time, wherever groups of people have lived together, they have also fought among themselves. Some have fought for control of basic necessities—food, water, and shelter—or territory. Others have been spurred to fight by religious differences. Still others have fought solely for sport. Throughout the ages, some fighters have taken up arms willingly. Others have been forced into battle. For all, however, the ultimate goal has always been victory.

OPPOSITE: Fierce Japanese warriors called samurai were known for their intense loyalty to their masters.

OPPOSITE Samurai are among the most successful and enduring warriors the world has ever known.

In Japan, samurai warriors fought at the command of their masters for control of land and territory. For more than 700 years, they slashed, shot, and pierced their way across battlefields. Yet, when not engaged in violent conflict, samurai led quiet, contemplative lives. They lived by a code that required extreme self-discipline and respect for others. This discipline and peace penetrated all aspects of their lives, for samurai knew that the day would come when they might be asked to die for their master. When that moment came, they wanted to face death in the same way they faced life—with calm understanding and courage.

The Rise of the Warrior

Samurai began to dominate the Japanese landscape in the 12th century, at a time when powerful families ruled Europe and Africa and a sophisticated culture thrived in Asia. Asian nations followed complex political systems, and religious practices such as **Shintoism**, **Buddhism**, and **Confucianism** dominated all ways of life.

OPPOSITE: Samurai had very distinct uniforms, weapons, and a code of conduct that touched every part of their life.

On the mainland, Asia's different cultures mixed through vast trading networks, and Asians exchanged goods and thoughts with Europeans and Africans. But because Japan was an island nation, it missed out on most of these connections. It remained relatively isolated from the rest of the world.

Japan did have some contact with China, however, and over the centuries, the Chinese influenced Japanese culture, bringing Buddhism to the island in the sixth century. A distinct Japanese culture and way of life emerged around the eighth century. The Japanese ruling regime also adopted a Chinese-style political system with a strong **central government** led by an emperor. However, by the late 12th century, the central government was corrupt and weakened.

In 1185, a powerful military leader named Yoritomo (1147–99) forced the emperor to give him the title of shogun, or "barbarian-conquering supreme general." The shogun became the ruler of the country, while the emperor was relegated to a solely ceremonial role. Japan was then divided into a number of large estates, most of which were given tax-free to rich and powerful men known as daimyo.

Power filtered down through the shogun to the daimyo. As peasant farmers—who now bore the brunt of the country's tax burden—struggled to eke out a living, they had no choice but to sell their land to the already rich daimyo, who gained control of larger and larger tracts of land. Each daimyo ruled over his own section of land. As a result, order was difficult to maintain. Roving bands of rebels stirred up trouble by **ransacking** the castles of daimyo, destroying crops, conquering lands, and preying upon people traveling the country's trade routes. Eventually, daimyo turned to independent warriors for protection, and the age of the samurai was born.

Samurai—which means "one who serves"—first acted as guards for the daimyo. Violent battles between daimyo over territory were common, as land suitable for agricultural development was in short supply. Daimyo needed samurai to help them retain their lands as well as to fight to obtain new territory. Organized samurai armies soon became a necessary component of Japanese

Samurai were ready to serve at a moment's notice.

Early Fighters

Although samurai are the best-known warriors from Japanese history, they were by no means the first fighters to emerge in Japan. Centuries-old accounts tell the first stories of warriors who embraced characteristics that later would become common among samurai. The *Nihongi* (*Chronicles of Japan*) mentions the use of archers on horseback in a seventh-century battle, which possibly became an early model for samurai. Some of the earliest fighters in Japan were the Yamato people, who came to the country from the Korean peninsula around the year 250. They rode on horseback, carried steel swords, and wore iron armor.

society. As their services were needed more and more, samurai's influence grew, and they soon became an important aristocratic class.

Despite their position of importance in Japanese society, most samurai lived simply. Their masters provided them with food and shelter. Samurai either lived in the same castle as their daimyo or nearby in the same village. If a daimyo had much land and therefore hundreds of samurai, the warriors might be scattered throughout his land in different castles. Occasionally, samurai became rich if their daimyo granted them a piece of land or if they married a woman from a wealthy family. In that case, they ruled over peasants, farmers, and merchants.

Daimyo often called on their samurai to spend weeks or months away from home, fighting to acquire land in faraway places. When they weren't away in battle, samurai spent time at home with their families. Samurai married, but usually not for love. Instead, marriages between samurai and women were arranged, often by a daimyo or higher-ranking samurai. The brides might be daughters of samurai. Poorer samurai did not have to marry a woman from a samurai family. They could marry common villagers. If a bride's parents were rich, they gave the samurai money so the couple could start a good life together.

Whether rich or poor, samurai sported a unique look. They draped themselves in flowing robes, called kimonos. Richer samurai wore kimonos made of silk. These robes featured neutral tones. A samurai's wife wore the same colors as her husband. Children were allowed to wear more colorful outfits, but these grew more subdued as they reached adulthood. Elderly samurai clad themselves

DESPITE THEIR POSITION OF IMPORTANCE IN JAPANESE SOCIETY, MOST SAMURAI LIVED SIMPLY.

in grays and browns to reflect their quiet, dignified ways. Underneath their kimonos, samurai wore loose trousers. They finished the look with a jacket draped over their kimono. Samurai wore their hair long in the back but shaved in the front. Then they pulled their hair into a knot at the top of their heads. Moustaches and beards were also important, as they symbolized manhood.

The central focus of a samurai's life was the bushido code. This code—a set of **morals**— stressed loyalty to one's master, self-discipline, and living in a respectful,

Samurai were required to be in control of their thoughts and actions at all times.

polite manner. A samurai was not to argue, yell, or drink excessive amounts of alcohol. He was to treat women with respect. The bushido code also stressed the importance of education. A samurai warrior relied on more than just his physical strength. He was also to be a smart, well-rounded man, well-versed in all aspects of life. Samurai studied many different subjects, including poetry, art, dancing, and mathematics.

In whatever a samurai did, the bushido code stressed that he must always think about death. This preoccupation with death was meant to prepare a samurai

Men of Many Names

A samurai gathered many names during his lifetime. At birth, he was anointed with a name that indicated good fortune. He might also be known by one of many common household nicknames. For example, the eldest son in a household was known as "Taro." At his coming-of-age ceremony, a samurai received his first adult name. These names generally were considered "gifts" from well-known and powerful people. The Japanese language revolves around characters, and receiving a character that was part of an important person's name was considered a great gift. As they grew older, samurai might change their own names to mark a particular event or to gain political favor.

for battle, for a samurai warrior faced the prospect of a violent and painful death at a young age. A samurai was honored to fight, wanting to prove his loyalty and devotion to his daimyo. An even greater honor was to die on the battlefield. Fighting nobly to the death—facing it calmly and without hysterics— was a respected way to meet one's end.

Because of the dignified manner in which samurai conducted themselves, they were held in high regard by the Japanese public. As samurai culture took firmer hold, the samurai's status continued to rise. Eventually, the samurai became a high, respected class—the warrior class. Only samurai were allowed to carry weapons, and they could kill anyone who disrespected them.

A Vicious Way to Fight

A samurai's weapons did not serve simply as tools to inflict injury. Weapons were a part of his soul. A samurai treated his weapons with the utmost respect. Bushido code did not allow a samurai to draw his weapon when not at war. To do so was considered rude and disrespectful.

OPPOSITE: Full-body armor protected a samurai from most enemy blows.

The sword was the samurai's most important weapon. According to legend, a samurai's spirit resided within his sword. He never let it leave his side. He might even sleep with it under his pillow at night. When a samurai entered a home, bushido code demanded that he leave his weapons at the door. But he might carry a small sword at his side at all times, reluctant to become totally unarmed in case danger might arise.

Swordsmiths, too, looked upon weapons with respect. Before starting work, the swordsmith prayed and bathed.

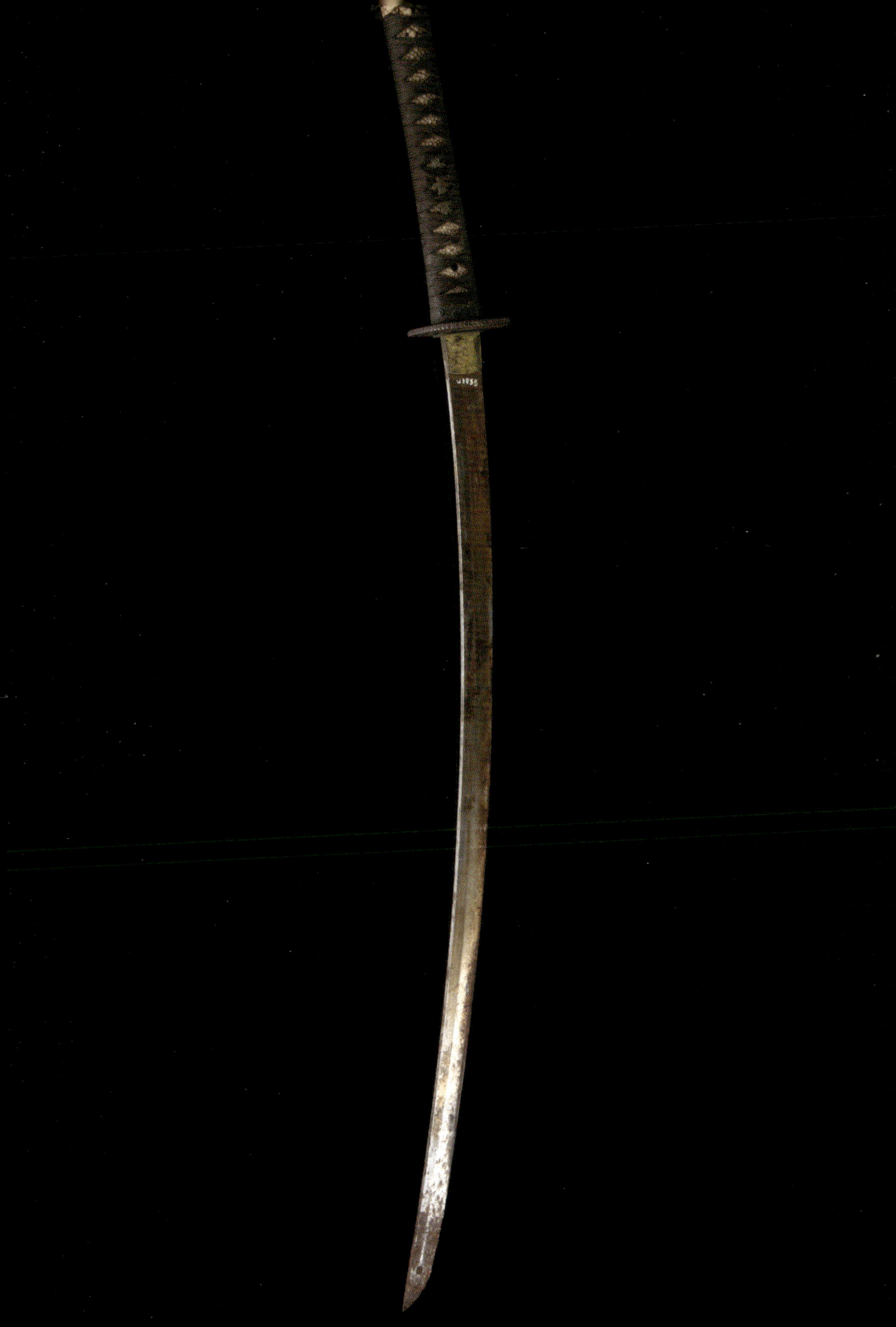

He clothed himself all in white and went about making swords in a quiet, respectful manner, almost like a priest. Swordsmiths relied on ancient rituals and old family techniques in their work. In order to curve a sword's blade, swordsmiths heated iron to high temperatures, then quickly dipped it into a pool of cool water, where it was bent. The best swordsmiths folded the slumped iron over and over again in the fire, creating a remarkably strong weapon.

The samurai's long, curved sword—the *katana*—developed from swords early warriors saw northern fighters use. Until then, warriors had carried a traditional straight sword. But samurai noticed how the curved blade inflicted deeper and more severe cuts when thrust into a man from on horseback. Samurai tended to use downward or horizontal motions when wielding their swords. A samurai also carried a smaller sword—the *wakizashi*—which was not used in fighting but instead served to cut off an opponent's head for proof of victory.

Although the sword was the samurai's favored weapon, he also used other weapons on the battlefield. Bows and arrows were used to cause injury from a long range—up to about 165 feet (50 meters). Usually, samurai fired arrows from behind a big, portable bamboo wall at the front lines, but a skilled rider might also fire from atop his galloping horse.

The spear became a popular weapon in the 15th century as battlefield skirmishes grew more organized. Spears were often more effective than long swords against samurai who used a modified katana designed especially for riding horseback. Samurai also used a chain with heavy weights at both ends for defense against swords.

Armed with spears, swords, or no weapons at all, samurai were fierce fighters.

Once a weapon became tangled in the chain, a samurai could easily disarm his opponent.

The *tessen* also proved to be an effective weapon. This folding iron fan could be carried discreetly in a samurai's belt. But unfolded, it could cause serious harm. The tessen was used mostly in self-defense—to knock an opponent's weapon from his hands. Rarely would a tessen alone inflict death or serious injury. In contrast, a pointed metal bar also used as a weapon could pierce through armor, quickly causing mortal wounds.

In the mid-16th century, European explorers introduced the **matchlock rifle** to Japan. Samurai adopted this weapon, which they called the *teppo*. On the battlefield, those firing teppo positioned themselves along the front lines, near the archers. A *teppo-taisho*, or rifle commander, led teppo squadrons. The *teppo-taisho* tried to create a constant rate of fire, using many warriors.

While the wives of samurai did not undergo formal weapons training, they sometimes were called upon to defend their homes if their husbands were away in battle. Women didn't use traditional weapons but carried a subtle emergency weapon: a hairpin. Japanese women used hairpins—some 6 inches (15 centimeters) long—to hold their long hair in place on top of their heads. In an emergency, the hairpin could be pulled out and inflict serious injury upon an enemy.

To protect himself from the onslaught of weapons attacks, a samurai dressed in an all encompassing suit of armor that consisted of many different iron plates connected by colorful silk strings. Dressing in full battle armor was a complex and multistep process. First, the samurai donned his **breechcloth**. Then he pulled on his kimono and cinched it around his waist. From there, he stepped into loose trousers. He pulled these tight around his waist and ankles using drawstrings; his pants appeared to billow around his legs.

With his undergarments in place, the samurai was ready to put on his armor. Over the trousers, shin guards protected the samurai's lower legs. Thigh guards served the same purpose on his upper legs. He pulled metal sleeves over his arms. Then he put on the largest piece of armor, a chest plate, which went over his chest and legs.

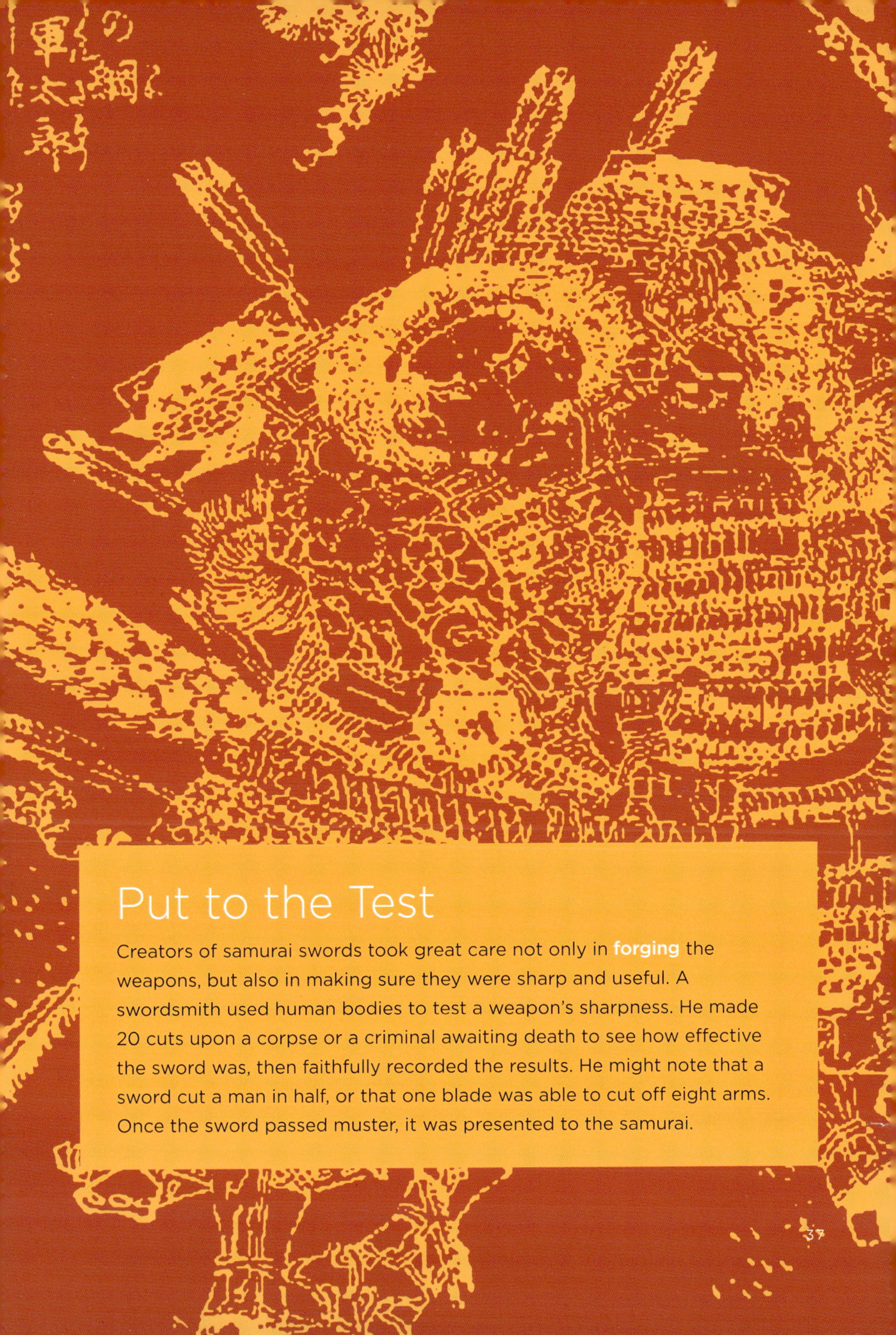

Put to the Test

Creators of samurai swords took great care not only in **forging** the weapons, but also in making sure they were sharp and useful. A swordsmith used human bodies to test a weapon's sharpness. He made 20 cuts upon a corpse or a criminal awaiting death to see how effective the sword was, then faithfully recorded the results. He might note that a sword cut a man in half, or that one blade was able to cut off eight arms. Once the sword passed muster, it was presented to the samurai.

The legs piece was split so he could easily sit astride his horse. Shoulder guards went on top of the chest plate to shield the samurai from arrows.

At each hip, the samurai tucked a sword into his belt. An iron collar protected his vulnerable throat. Before he placed his helmet on his head, he tied on a soft cotton cap and put on his face mask, or *mempo*. Adorned with grotesque and fearsome features, such as arched eyebrows and a scowling mouth, the mempo not only protected the samurai and helped to keep his helmet

Supply and Demand

Samurai armies needed supplies, such as food, while stationed on battlefronts both near and far from home. The daimyo was responsible for gathering and transporting the supplies needed to feed his samurai and horses. Because Japan's hilly terrain was not suitable for wheeled transport, daimyo often required samurai and animals to form supply chains on foot. Samurai carefully protected these supply lines, for if supplies ran out, battles had to be cut short. At times, rather than trying to transport the great number of supplies needed, daimyo ordered their samurai to take over villages, where peasants were forced to give them food.

secure, but it also served to frighten the enemy. The helmet, too, was decorated with intricate and fantastical designs such as horns, dragons, or other creatures. These designs were supposed to strike fear into opponents; they also identified the warrior and his family. Most helmets featured a small hole at the top to provide both ventilation and a place for the samurai's topknot.

Japanese armor was lighter than the bulky armor worn by European knights. This allowed for ease of movement, especially in the hand-to-hand combat favored by samurai. The lightweight uniform also provided more comfort in Japan's sometimes warm weather, but it wasn't always effective in protecting a samurai against heavy blows.

Ready for Attack

Samurai fought on two fronts: the fort and the battlefield. Samurai commonly traveled to an enemy fort or castle and laid **siege** to it. Early forts were made of wood and were therefore particularly vulnerable to fire. To attack stone castles, armies would try to break down walls or **catapult** large stones over the walls. A samurai army usually tried to cut off the food or water supply to a fort, which often ended in the fort's surrender.

OPPOSITE: Attacking a Japanese castle sometimes required samurai to cross a wide, water-filled ditch called a moat.

On the battlefield, opposing samurai armies lined up across from one another, each samurai astride his horse. Then the samurai charged, firing arrows while galloping toward their opponents. This required great skill. Once the opposing armies got close enough for hand-to-hand combat, the fighters dismounted their horses and challenged one another to individual swordfights.

In the 13th century, the samurai fighting style changed after the Japanese suffered two attacks from Mongol invaders. The Mongols (a people from mainland Asia) fought in highly organized groups and outnumbered the Japanese, nearly defeating them the first time. In the second battle, a typhoon blew in from the sea, eliminating the Mongol enemy and saving the Japanese from defeat.

After the Mongol invasion, the samurai realized that they needed organized armies and coordinated attacks in order to be strong in war. They recognized that their bow-and-arrow tactics no longer guaranteed success. As a result, samurai became more dependent upon their swords and spears in battle. Instead of firing arrows from a long range, samurai warriors rode close to their enemy on horseback to inflict serious injury or death with the sword.

Samurai fighting style changed again in the 16th century with the introduction of the European musket. The Japanese admired this gun and adapted it for use in their battles. A few years after the gun's introduction into Japanese society, samurai armies were relying heavily upon the weapon, and soon Japanese gunsmiths were producing large quantities of firearms.

Samurai armies looked to their daimyo as the head of their army. He planned attacks, who would fight, and

Way of the Sword

The samurai fighting style lives on today in the martial art of kendo, which means "way of the sword." Girls and boys in Japan practice kendo in gym class, and kendo tournaments are held around the world. Participants use a bamboo sword and strike one of four parts of an opponent's body—the top of the head, the wrist, the ribs, or the throat, scoring points for each hit. Fighters wear armor to protect themselves. Matches are lively, swift, and loud, but—unlike in a samurai battle—everyone leaves with his or her life and limbs intact.

who would stay behind to defend his property. Daimyo generally accompanied their samurai to battle, but they stayed at the back of the battlefield to give orders, protected by a large number of bodyguards.

The daimyo's orders filtered down to a second layer of samurai leadership. A daimyo's relatives—sons, grandsons, brothers-in-law, uncles—or trusted advisors held secondary leadership positions and were called *hatamoto* (officers). The officers in turn ruled over samurai called *go-kenin* (loyal followers). Sometimes samurai recruited peasants, called *ashigaru*, to fight in their army for a limited time. A samurai's rank within the army usually was based on how much land he controlled. If he was able to obtain more land through war or marriage, he might move up in rank.

Samurai training started early, when boys from samurai families were around seven years old. They studied closely with samurai and learned valuable subjects such as reading and writing. They also started to train in martial arts and played games that emphasized quick thinking and strategy. A young samurai studied under a more experienced samurai. The bond between teacher and student ran deep and was called *shudo*, or *bido*. Shudo was very important, as it was the way samurai tradition was passed down from one generation to the next. The devotion the samurai teacher and student expressed for each other was nearly as deep as the loyalty they expressed to their daimyo masters.

A samurai teacher might come upon his young charge at the most unexpected moments and surprise him with the strike of a stick. This taught the hopeful warrior that he must always be on guard. When practicing weaponry, the focus was on perfect form. Young students first practiced with wooden sticks. Using weapons was more than a physical pursuit. Students also learned to focus their minds on the task. Between the ages of 12 and 18, students took part in a coming-of-age ceremony called *genbuku*, in which they received their sword, said goodbye to their family, and chose a new name.

Samurai trained not only in physical skills but also in psychological skills. The mind of a samurai required toughness and mental **agility**, which he worked to develop throughout his life. To do this, the samurai spent time in quiet contemplation, thinking about death. He used techniques of **Zen** discipline to quiet his mind and control his fears. This taught him to be rational and use his mind, for if he acted unreasonably in war and made rash decisions, the results could be disastrous. Great dishonor fell upon the samurai who faced certain defeat on the battlefield. In this case, many samurai chose to commit suicide rather than meet shame, capture, or inevitable loss.

A samurai's suicide was particularly gruesome. The preferred method of taking his own life was to slice his belly. This action, known as seppuku (or hara-kiri), was first noted in the 12th century. Samurai believed that their spirits resided within their stomachs, and killing themselves in this manner was thought to be the quickest way to die. Eventually, seppuku came to be seen as a brave way to die and was reserved only for samurai.

Over time, the seppuku ritual evolved and became quite elaborate. The samurai, clad in white, knelt upon a white cushion. He grasped a sword and brought it to his belly, then cut lengthwise, from left to right. A close friend stood behind him—his job was to cut the samurai's head off to lessen the samurai's suffering. Although samurai

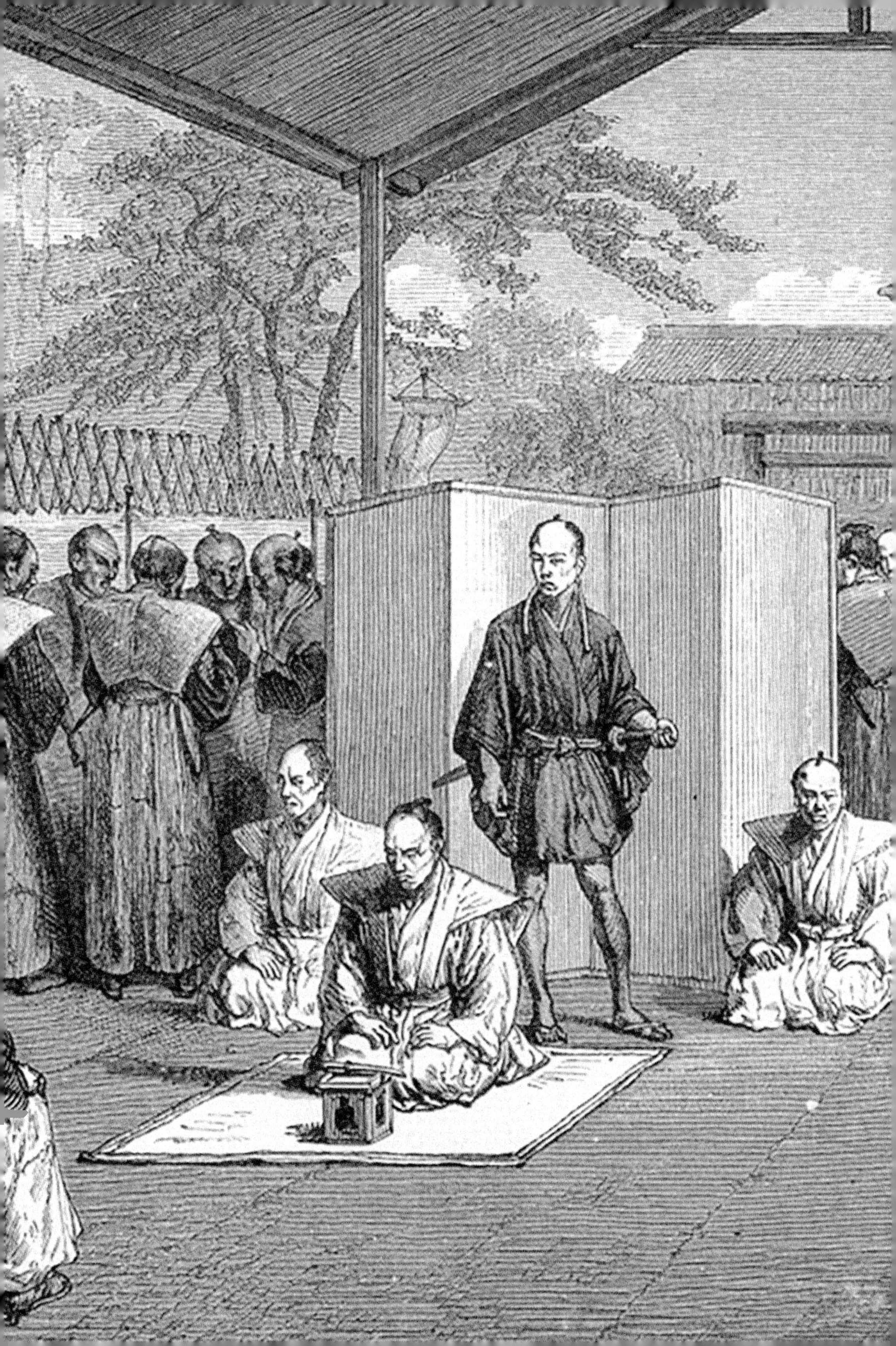

Life and Death

The samurai obsession with death is easier to understand after one takes a closer look at the conditions in which samurai lived. They, along with all the people of Japan, faced hardship on a daily basis. Natural disasters such as earthquakes, floods, and torrential rains wiped out crops and farm animals, and often resulted in human death. Without a food supply, the people faced famine regularly. No one understood disease or how the human body worked, so illness frequently claimed young lives. Because they saw death all around, samurai grew to appreciate the fleeting beauty of life.

who were defeated in battle often chose to commit suicide of their own accord, others were forced to kill themselves as punishment for a crime. Some samurai chose to commit suicide if their lord died in battle. Samurai might also perform seppuku to persuade a lord to change his ways if all other negotiations had failed.

A samurai who failed in battle or failed to protect his daimyo was a dishonored samurai. If he didn't commit suicide, the failed samurai roamed the land and became a beggar, looked down upon by all. He had lost his honor and respect. Without those two things, he was no longer considered a samurai.

The Bravest and the Best

Successful samurai warriors were noted for their courage and bravery and earned an honored place in society. They were like today's rock stars or professional athletes, revered by many. Tales of their exploits filtered down from generation to generation, and their legendary actions remain important stories in Japanese history and culture.

OPPOSITE: Unlike Japan's shadowy fighters called ninjas, samurai were well known and openly celebrated by the public.

One well-known samurai tale relates the story of Oda Nobunaga (1534–82), who rose to power at a time when chaos and **anarchy** ruled Japan. At the time, the country was split into a number of small factions, each ruled by powerful daimyo, who were constantly at war with each other. Nobunaga was born to a minor lord who was always fighting to gain land and power. Nobunaga rose through the samurai army ranks, first by establishing control of his own warring family, then by controlling and defeating neighboring provinces. One of Nobunaga's first stunning victories came in 1560, when he defeated a rival clan in the battle of Okehazama despite the fact that his army of 5,000 was greatly outnumbered. Soon after, Nobunaga built himself into a powerful leader and warrior with one overarching goal: to unite Japan and become leader of the entire country.

Art Subjects

Due to the dramatic nature of their lives, samurai make compelling subjects for art, and the chaos, wars, heroes, and villains of Japanese history have long been recorded through paintings and woodblock prints. Renowned artist Tsukioka Yoshitoshi (1839–92) glorified the tale of the 47 ronin (masterless samurai) through a series of illustrated biographies in 1869. Other frequently depicted samurai subjects include the famous swordsman Miyamoto Musashi (1584–1645) and female warriors such as Han Gaku (c. 1200). Such art has helped to provide a lasting record of these fighters and to bolster their honored place in Japanese society.

In order to accomplish this, though, Nobunaga had to get rid of those who opposed him, including the country's Buddhist monks. Nobunaga was fascinated by Christianity and welcomed missionaries to the island. This fondness for Christianity put him at odds with the monks, who were powerful because peasants tended to identify with them. Afraid that the monks might lead an army against him, Nobunaga sought to eliminate them. In 1571, he and his army attacked a monastery at Mount Hiei, killing those who refused to surrender. Some historians believe that around 3,000 people—monks, nuns, and their family members—were killed that day.

Throughout his career, Nobunaga helped to change the way samurai fought. Guns had just been introduced by **Westerners**, and Nobunaga trained himself and others on how to best use them in battle. He also built strong stone fortresses that could withstand gunfire. Nobunaga was close to his goal of uniting the country when his two top generals, upset over the way he had been treating them, turned against him and killed him in 1582.

Unlike Nobunaga's generals, many samurai throughout history distinguished themselves by their loyalty to their daimyo. A legend of such loyalty is the tale of the 47 ronin, or masterless samurai. The story begins in 1701, when a daimyo named Lord Asano (1667–1701) went to visit the shogun, Tokugawa Tsunayoshi (1646–1709). Also in attendance was another daimyo, Lord Kira (c. 1600s–1703), who insulted Asano. Angered, Asano lost his temper and, in a fit of rage, drew his sword and attempted to kill Kira. Because Kira was well-respected, tradition dictated that Asano commit seppuku. As a result, his samurai became ronin.

After Asano's death, the ronin carefully plotted their revenge on Kira, waiting almost a year to catch him by surprise. Finally, on January 30, 1703, they ambushed Kira at his house and forced him into an outhouse, where they killed him and cut off his head. They also killed several of Kira's samurai. The ronin, ranging in age from 15 to 77, were forced to commit seppuku because of the murders. They were buried with Lord Asano, and their graves remain a popular tourist attraction in the Sengakuji Temple in Tokyo.

Over the years, some people have praised the ronin as brave warriors who upheld the bushido code by seeking revenge on the man who was responsible for their master's death. Others have viewed the situation

Saigo Takamori

differently. They point to the fact that the ronin spent a year planning the attack in order to guarantee success and argue that samurai following true bushido code would have attacked right away and not waited for sure success.

More than 100 years after the 47 ronin incident, Saigo Takamori (1827–77), one of Japan's most influential—and last—samurai arose. Even though he had been born a low-level samurai, Takamori quickly rose through the military ranks to take command of Japan's large national army, which attempted to wrestle control away from the shogun and place it back in the emperor's hands. In 1868, Takamori led the army to victory over the shogun in the Boshin War, leaving the emperor in control. Although he held an official post loyal to the emperor, Takamori disliked the West's influence over Japan. He also wanted to go to war with Korea because Korean officials failed to recognize Japan's emperor as head of state. Other leaders opposed the plan, and Takamori, disenchanted with the government's central power, resigned. However, he was well-respected, and a number of samurai followed him to his hometown, where he opened an academy for samurai training.

In 1877, Takamori and his followers revolted against the government because officials instituted a number of reforms unfavorable to samurai. For one, samurai were no longer allowed to carry their weapons. In addition, the government stopped the centuries-old practice of requiring farmers to provide rice **stipends** to the samurai. Takamori's revolt, called the Satsuma Rebellion, pitted his army against the imperial army. Although Takamori's samurai waged war against the imperial army for several months, the rebellion was ultimately unsuccessful. Takamori was badly injured in the final battle, and legend says that he committed seppuku.

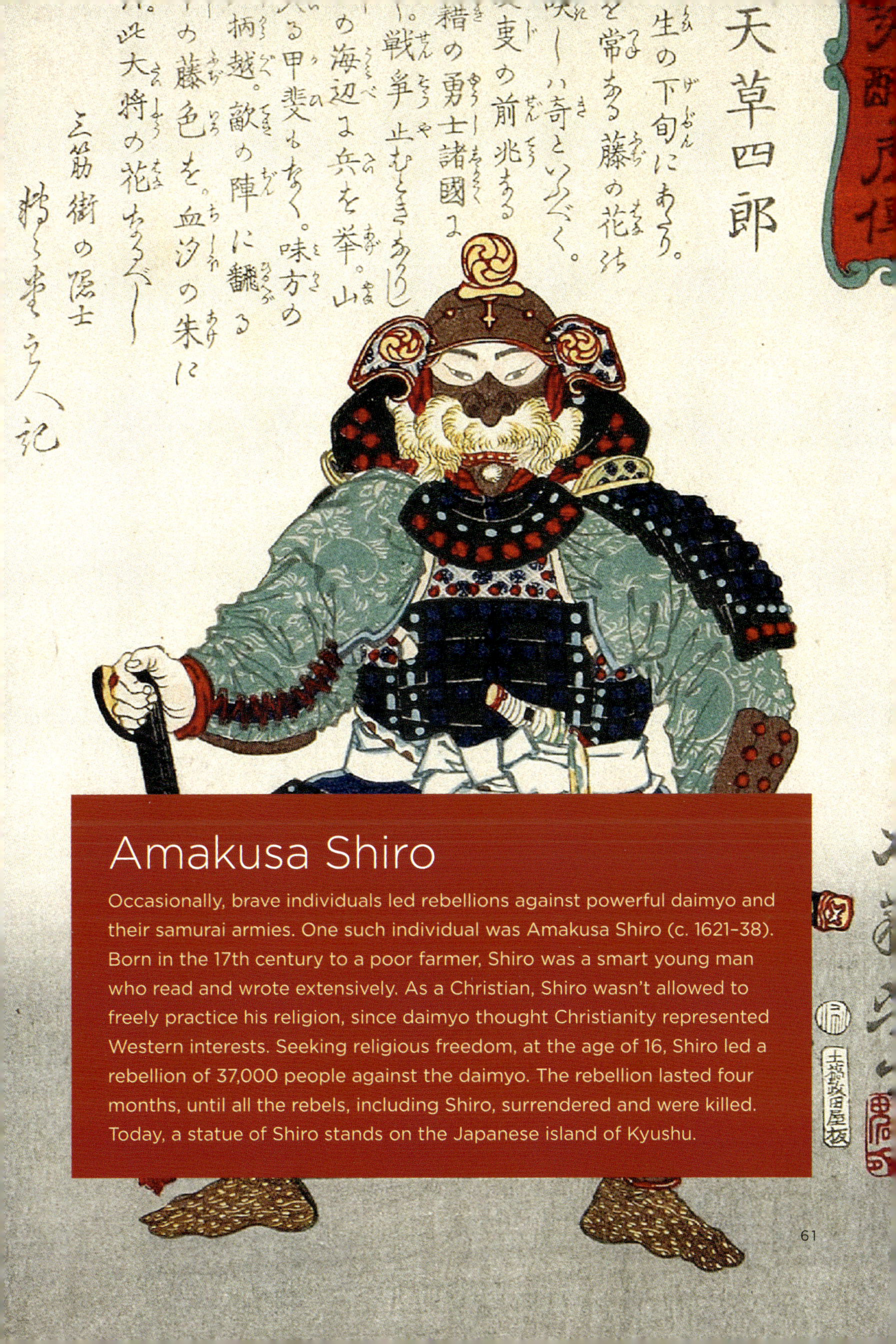

Amakusa Shiro

Occasionally, brave individuals led rebellions against powerful daimyo and their samurai armies. One such individual was Amakusa Shiro (c. 1621–38). Born in the 17th century to a poor farmer, Shiro was a smart young man who read and wrote extensively. As a Christian, Shiro wasn't allowed to freely practice his religion, since daimyo thought Christianity represented Western interests. Seeking religious freedom, at the age of 16, Shiro led a rebellion of 37,000 people against the daimyo. The rebellion lasted four months, until all the rebels, including Shiro, surrendered and were killed. Today, a statue of Shiro stands on the Japanese island of Kyushu.

He's considered a great hero in Japanese history for revolting against the government and Western influence.

Although most samurai were male, sometimes female samurai fought alongside their warrior husbands. Just like men, if they fell into dishonor, they were expected to commit seppuku. One legendary female samurai was Tomoe Gozen (c. 1161–84), who served in the divisive Gempei War from 1180 to 1185. The war pitted two rival clans—the Minamoto and the Taira—against each other. Gozen led part of the Minamoto army and participated in battle as fully as any male samurai. Many women of this time could skillfully wield a spear, but Gozen was also skilled in the use of the bow and arrow. Known for her bravery, Gozen often completed dangerous scouting missions. She died on the battlefield, and her heroic death makes Gozen one of Japan's most endearing cultural figures to this day.

End of an Era

Before the samurai era formally ended in 1867, the need for such warriors had already been declining for a couple hundred years. Intense fighting took place between warring daimyo in the 15th and 16th centuries, but by the end of the 16th century, a number of important rulers managed to unite the country. For the next three centuries, Japan experienced a time of relative peace, and the need for the samurai's fighting ways lessened.

U.S. Navy Commodore Matthew Perry

Samurai retained their importance as members of Japan's higher class. However, instead of fighting, many took jobs as **bureaucrats** for their daimyo. By the 18th and early 19th centuries, they carried their swords as a symbol of status but rarely needed to use them. They still held the power to kill anyone who disrespected them, but few appear to have taken advantage of this right. Samurai continued to live by the bushido code and heavily emphasized values such as education and respect. If anything, samurai even more closely followed bushido since they spent little time fighting. They formalized the code and urged the rest of Japanese society to follow its principles. With their extra time, samurai also pursued roles as learned scholars.

The beginning of the end for the samurai can be traced to 1853. In July of that year, U.S. Navy

Commodore Matthew Perry (1794–1858) guided four ships into the harbor at Edo (modern-day Tokyo). Perry led an American expedition to find out more about this mysterious island nation. Until this point, Japan had managed to stay mostly isolated from the rest of the world. The country engaged in only limited trade with the West, and shoguns closely controlled any contact with foreigners.

The United States, however, wanted to open trade with Japan. Perry threatened to declare war against

the country unless those in power agreed to open its lands to outsiders. As Japanese officials looked out into the harbor at giant American ships with large guns and cannons at the ready, they saw no other choice than to agree to Perry's demands. Even their most powerful samurai warriors would be no match for the heavy ammunition. By 1854, Japan agreed to allow U.S. officials into the country to explore and trade.

The era of isolation had ended. The world was now connected in a complex global network. In order to compete in this new world, Japan decided it needed a larger, more forceful army to guard itself against possible attacks. This army needed powerful, modern weapons to ensure success. Japan expanded its imperial army, drawing soldiers from all social classes. The samurai, with their suddenly old-fashioned weapons, were no longer in demand.

Samurai and daimyo rebelled against the government in the 1860s in an attempt to keep Western influence from infiltrating the country. Then, in 1868, Emperor Mutsuhito (1852–1912) restored order and claimed power, the first Japanese emperor in centuries to hold actual power. The way of life the Japanese had known for 700 years, with shoguns, daimyo, and samurai in control, suddenly ended. Samurai continued to stage rebellions, with the last recorded rebellion being Saigo Takamori's unsuccessful Satsuma Rebellion of 1877. The remaining samurai class, no longer holding any power, retreated into the background and faded from the spotlight, becoming only a shadowy representation of Japan's past.

Although samurai disappeared from society, their ways have not been forgotten. For hundreds of years, samurai have been immortalized in books and, in the last few decades, on television and the big screen.

In Japan, the TV series *Mito Komon*, set in the 17th century, details the travels of a disguised samurai who hunts down criminals. He and his samurai companions dispense justice, and good triumphs over evil. The late Japanese film director Akira Kurosawa regularly featured samurai-themed work. His style and storytelling skills, embodied in such films as *The Seven Samurai*, are emulated by movie directors all around the world.

Folded Gifts

The Japanese are famous for their origami—elaborate designs crafted out of folded paper. Origami figures were made for many occasions, such as weddings and other celebrations. In the early days, the bark of the mulberry tree was used to make origami. The bark was expensive, so only the wealthy practiced the craft. Samurai warriors gave pieces of origami to each other as gifts, representing good luck symbols in times of battle. Sometimes samurai created origami boxes to hold valuable items. Over time, origami was formed out of paper, bringing the art to the masses.

In Japanese literature, samurai take center stage in the 1980 book *The Samurai* by Shusako Endo. Based on a true story, the novel details the travels of samurai warriors who visit Mexico, accompanied by a Christian missionary priest. They reluctantly agree to convert to Christianity but face shame and persecution when they return home. Samurai remain central figures in Japanese comic books and **anime** series as well.

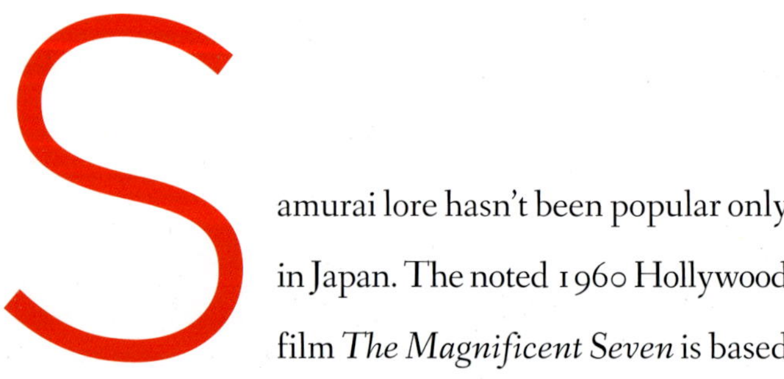

Samurai lore hasn't been popular only in Japan. The noted 1960 Hollywood film *The Magnificent Seven* is based

upon the Japanese movie *The Seven Samurai*. George Lucas, creator of the *Star Wars* movies, based his Jedi knights on samurai stories. In 2003, Hollywood released the movie *The Last Samurai*, a story loosely based on the experiences of Saigo Takamori. Although the film, which stars Tom Cruise, takes some dramatic license, it was a blockbuster. In books, American author James Clavell turned his avid interest in samurai into the 1975 novel *Shogun*, which explores the Japanese era when shoguns ruled the country, daimyo ruled their provinces, and samurai traveled and fought to defend their daimyo. The book sold seven million copies in its first five years, and a 1980 television miniseries drew 130 million viewers.

Although samurai no longer exist, their fighting styles and philosophies figure centrally in the Japanese way of life today. Japanese kamikaze pilots during World War II flew their planes into enemy positions to inflict damage or death. The kamikaze looked to the samurai and their fearless perception of death for inspiration. In Japanese business, the bushido code followed so rigidly by samurai still rules. For example, workers in large companies respect and revere their leaders and pledge outstanding loyalty, just as samurai pledged loyalty to their daimyo.

Samurai are symbolic of a time when Japanese daimyo wrestled each other for control of land and wealth, which resulted in violent, bloody battles. But samurai also symbolize a time of respect and honor. They've earned their place in history, and their influence is certain to reach many more generations.

What's for Dinner?

A samurai's diet relied heavily on rice, which was eaten with every meal. Samurai added vegetables such as potatoes, radishes, and yams to the rice. They might also come across nuts and beans. Since Japan is an island nation, samurai ate large amounts of fish, and even octopus, jellyfish, clams, and seaweed. The religions of Buddhism and Shintoism usually prohibited the eating of red meat, so this did not become common in Japan until the 19th century. For drinks, sake, made of fermented rice, was popular. Otherwise, samurai drank tea.

Selected Bibliography

Bajalan, Djene, and Patrick Needham. "The Myths and Realities of Life as a Samurai." KSMU Radio. April 4, 2024. https://www.ksmu.org/podcast/talking-history/2024-04-04/the-myths-and-realities-of-life-as-a-samurai.

Blair, Gavin. *An Illustrated Guide to Samurai History and Culture: From the Age of Musashi to Contemporary Pop Culture.* Tokyo; Rutland, Vt.: Tuttle Pub., 2022.

Cohen, Richard. *By the Sword: A History of Gladiators, Musketeers, Samurai, Swashbucklers, and Olympic Champions.* New York: Random House, 2002.

Germain, Jacquelyne. "Who Was Yasuke, Japan's First Black Samurai?" *Smithsonian* magazine. January 10, 2023. https://www.smithsonianmag.com/history/who-was-yasuke-japans-first-black-samurai-180981416.

Perry, Kevin E. G. "Shogun: How an Englishman from Kent Made an Extraordinary Journey to Become the First Western Samurai." *The Independent.* September 15, 2024. https://www.independent.co.uk/arts-entertainment/tv/features/shogun-true-story-cast-emmys-2024-b2613169.html.

Ribner, Susan, and Richard Chin. *The Martial Arts*. New York: Harper & Row, 1978.

Roach, Colin M. *Japanese Swords: Cultural Icons of a Nation: The History, Metallurgy, and Iconography of the Samurai Sword.* Tokyo; Rutland, Vt.: Tuttle Pub., 2010.

Glossary

agility the ability to move with quickness and grace

anarchy having no government; lawlessness and political disorder typically rule the land during times of anarchy

anime a type of Japanese animation that uses colorful graphics, vibrant characters, and action filled plots, often set in the future

aristocratic relating to a high social class that holds the power and privilege in some societies

breechcloth a samurai's undergarments, usually made of cotton and tied together with string, over which he wore his armor

Buddhism a religion of central and southern Asia based upon the teachings of Buddha, who lived around 500 BCE; Buddhism stresses overcoming suffering by mental concentration and living in a moral way

bureaucrat a person who serves in a government marked by an adherence to fixed rules, formalities, and rigid authority

catapult to throw an object over a wall or other barrier by use of a throwing mechanism that launches the object with great force

central government a ruling body, usually based in a capital city, that makes decisions for the whole country, instead of letting regional groups make their own laws

Confucianism a religion based upon the teachings of Confucius, a Chinese scholar who lived around 500 BCE; Confucianism is marked by living in a kindly way and respecting all people

forge to work with metal by melting it and then hammering it into a specific shape

matchlock rifle an early gun and one of the first to use a trigger; when the trigger was pulled, a lit fuse made contact with gunpowder and caused the gun to fire

moral a principle of right and wrong, especially relating to the teaching of proper behavior and living through good conduct

ransack to search thoroughly and often steal some things, destroying almost everything in sight in the process

Shintoism the first religion practiced in Japan; Shintoism combines a love of nature with a worship of ancestor spirits

siege to attack a fort or castle by surrounding it and threatening the people inside until they are forced to surrender

stipend a regular payment, usually in the form of food or money, for services or to help defray expenses

Westerner a person from the West, or the part of the world that includes the United States and Europe

Zen a philosophy and sect of the Buddhist religion characterized by the seeking of enlightenment through quiet, meditative practices

Websites

A Brief History of Samurai Warfare

https://www.historyextra.com/period/medieval/brief-history-samurai-warfare-battles-armour-myths-facts

Learn how samurai prepared for battle.

History of the Samurai

https://www.pbs.org/wgbh/nova/samurai/hist-nf.html

Explore a timeline of samurai history.

Yasuke

https://www.britannica.com/biography/Yasuke

Read about the African-born samurai named Yasuke.

Index

armor, 27, 34, 36, 38–39, 44
  helmets, 38–39
  mempo (face mask), 38–39
artwork, 55
battlefield tactics, 42–43, 45
  chain of command, 45
books, 69, 72, 73
Boshin War, 59
Buddhism, 13, 14, 55, 75
bushido code, 10, 21, 22, 23, 25, 27, 28, 57, 59, 65, 74
castle attacks, 41
China, 14
Christianity, 55, 61, 72
code of conduct. *See* bushido code
coming-of-age ceremony, 47
daimyo, 15, 16, 19, 20, 25, 39, 43, 45, 54, 56, 61, 63, 65, 68, 73, 74
death, 10, 23, 25, 47, 48, 50, 51, 74
dishonored samurai, 47, 51, 62
Emperor Mutsuhito, 68
female samurai, 62
fort attacks, 41
Gempei War, 62
Gozen, Tomoe, 62
horsemanship, 18, 30, 31, 38, 42, 43
kamikaze pilots, 73–74
kendo, 44
lifestyle, 10, 19–21, 22, 23, 25, 50, 65
  clothing, 20–21
  diet, 75
  hairstyles, 21
  marriage, 20
Lord Asano, 56–57
Lord, Kira, 56–57
Mongols, 42
Mount Hiei, 55
movies, 69, 72–73
names, 24
ninjas, 53
Nobunaga, Oda, 54–56
Okehazama, 54
origami, 70
Perry, Matthew, 64, 65–66, 67
ronin, 55, 56, 57, 59
Satsuma Rebellion, 60, 68
Sengakuji Temple, 57
seppuku (hara-kiri), 48, 51, 57, 60, 62
Shintoism, 13, 75
Shiro, Amakusa, 61
shoguns, 15, 56, 59, 66, 68, 73
suicide. *See* seppuku (hara-kiri)
supply lines, 39, 41
swordsmiths, 28, 30, 37
Takamori, Saigo, 58, 59, 60, 62, 68, 73
television shows, 69, 73
Tokyo, 57
training, 45–47, 56, 60
  shudo, 46
Tsunayoshi, Tokugawa, 56
uniforms, 6, 13
United States, 65, 66, 67
weapons
  bows and arrows, 31, 38, 42, 43, 62
  chains, 31, 34
  guns, 35, 43, 56, 67
  hairpins, 35
  spears, 31, 32, 43, 62
  swords, 28, 30–31, 32, 37, 38, 42, 43, 44, 47, 48, 65
  tessen, 34
Yamato people, 18
Yoritomo, 15
Zen, 47